Which is smaller?

Identify and circle the smaller object.

Which is shorter?

Identify and circle the shorter object.

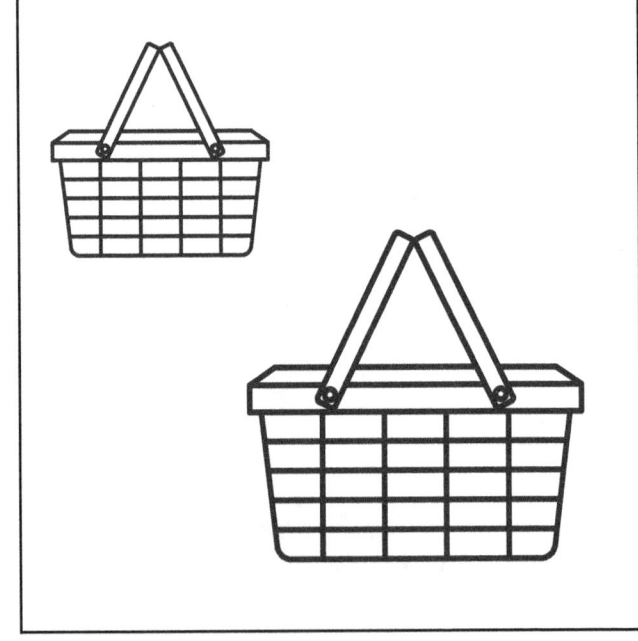

Order by weight

Order the images from lightest to heaviest.

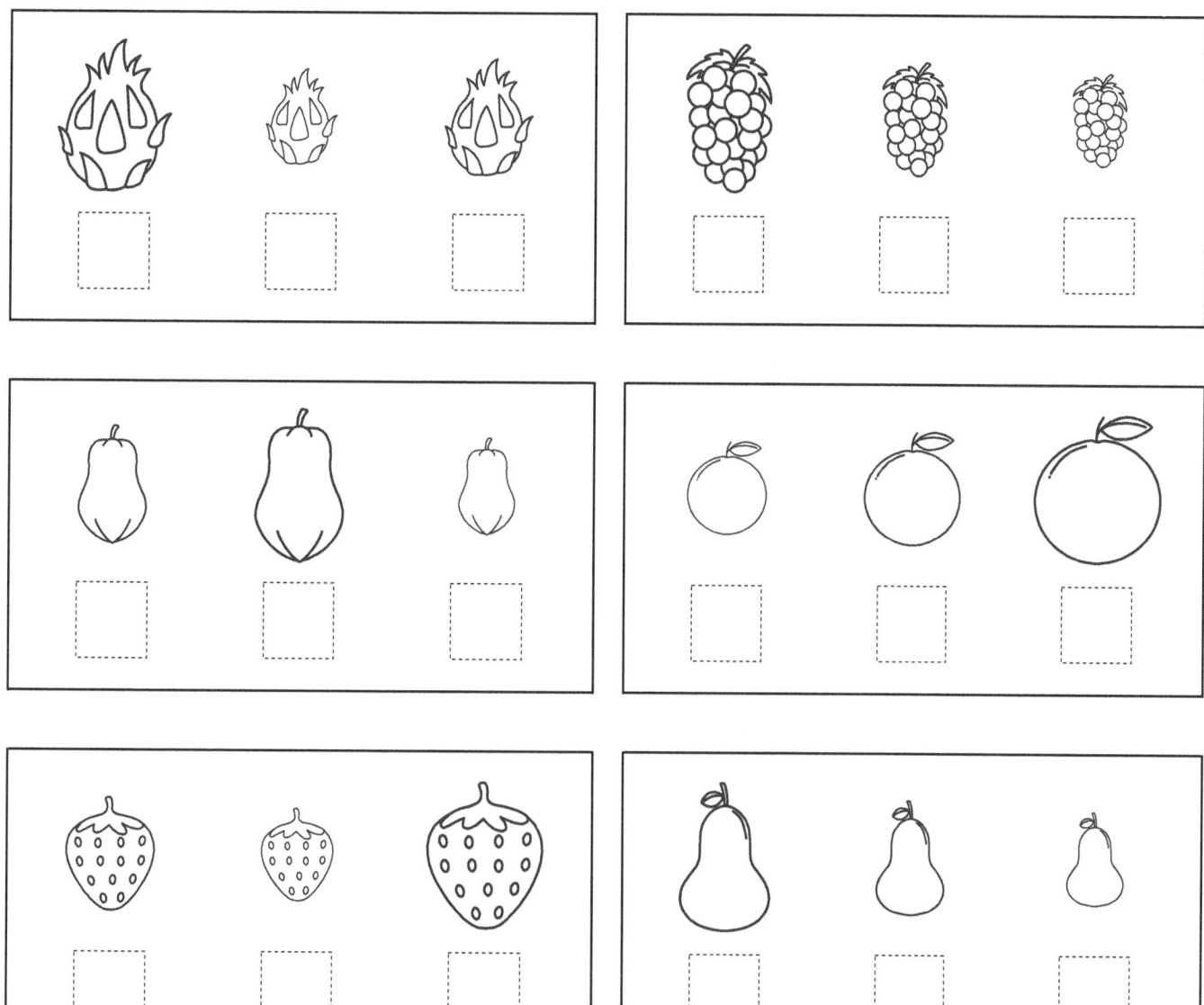

Which is lighter?

Identify and circle the lighter object.

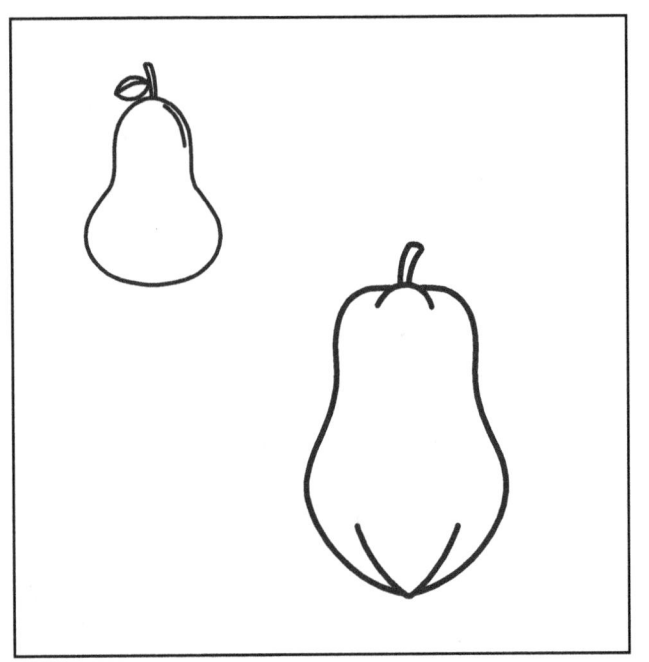

More vs less

Identify the collection that has more/less items.

Which is shorter?

Identify and circle the shorter object.

More vs less

Find the item that is more and item that is less.

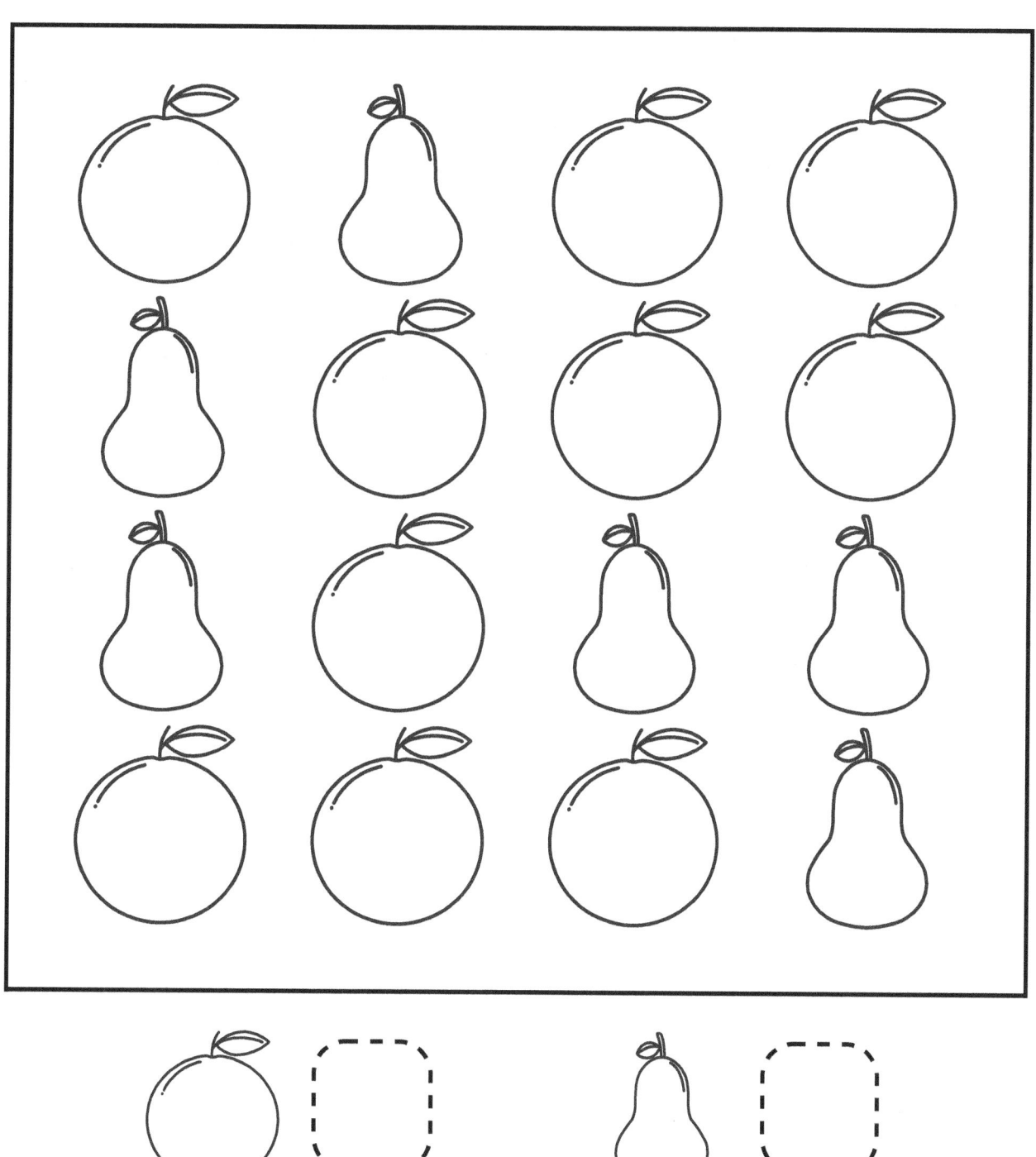

Order by length

Order from the shortest to longest object.

Order by length

Order from the shortest to longest object.

More vs less

Find the item that is more and item that is less.

1)

2)
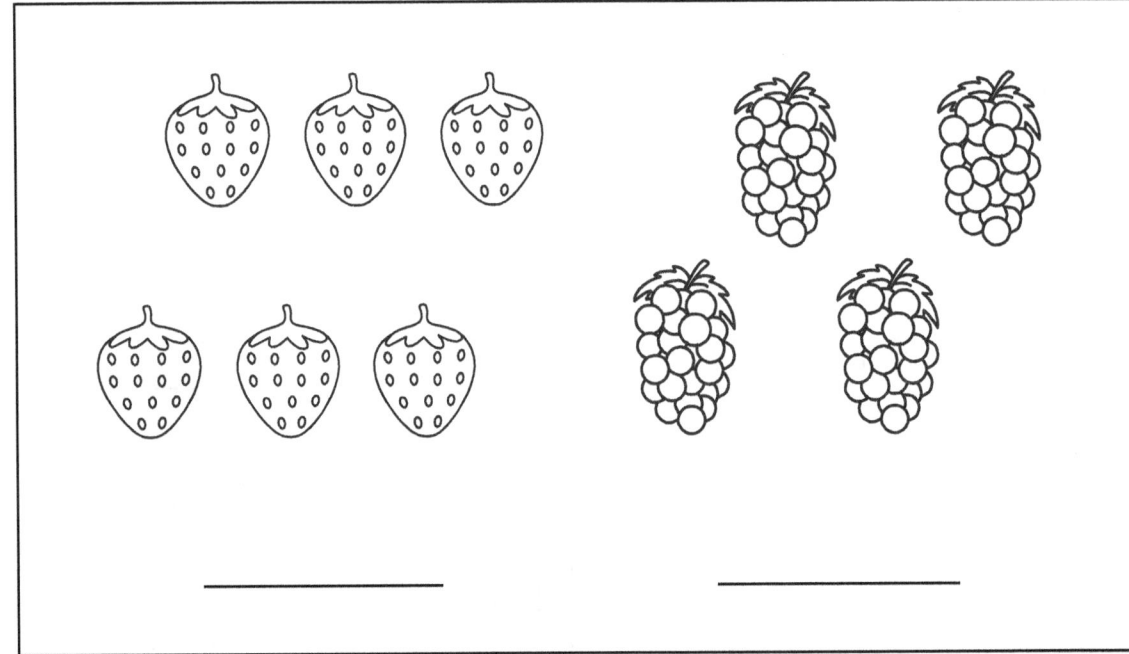

Identify the bigger object

Circle the bigger object.

Which is longer?

Identify and circle the longer object.

Longest and shortest

Circle the longest and cross out the shortest object.

Which is Heavier?

Identify and circle the heavier object.

Identify the smaller object

Circle the smaller object

More vs less

Find the item that is more and item that is less.

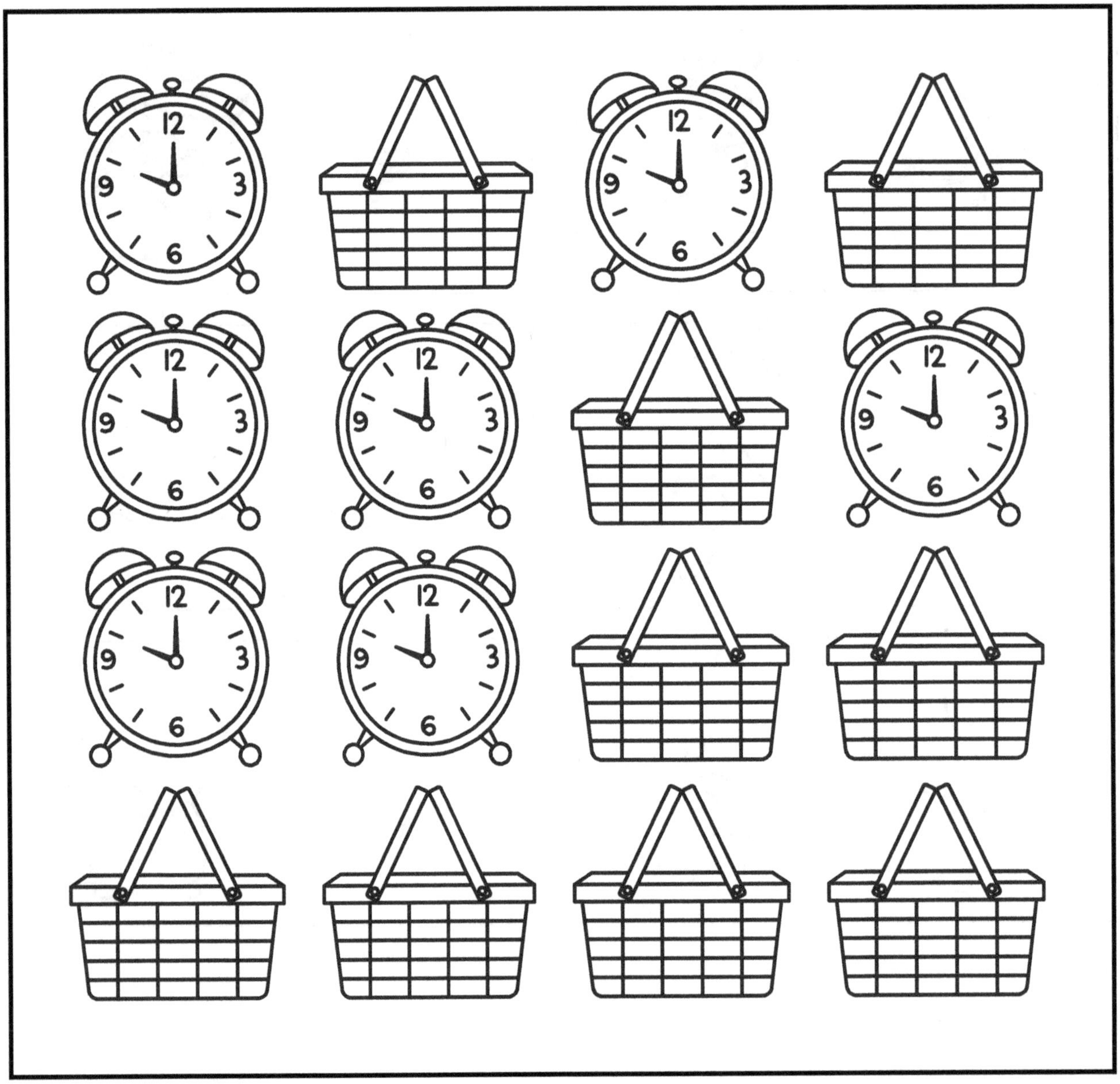

Which is heavier?

Identify and circle the heavier object.

Find the heaviest

Draw a rectangle around the heaviest image.

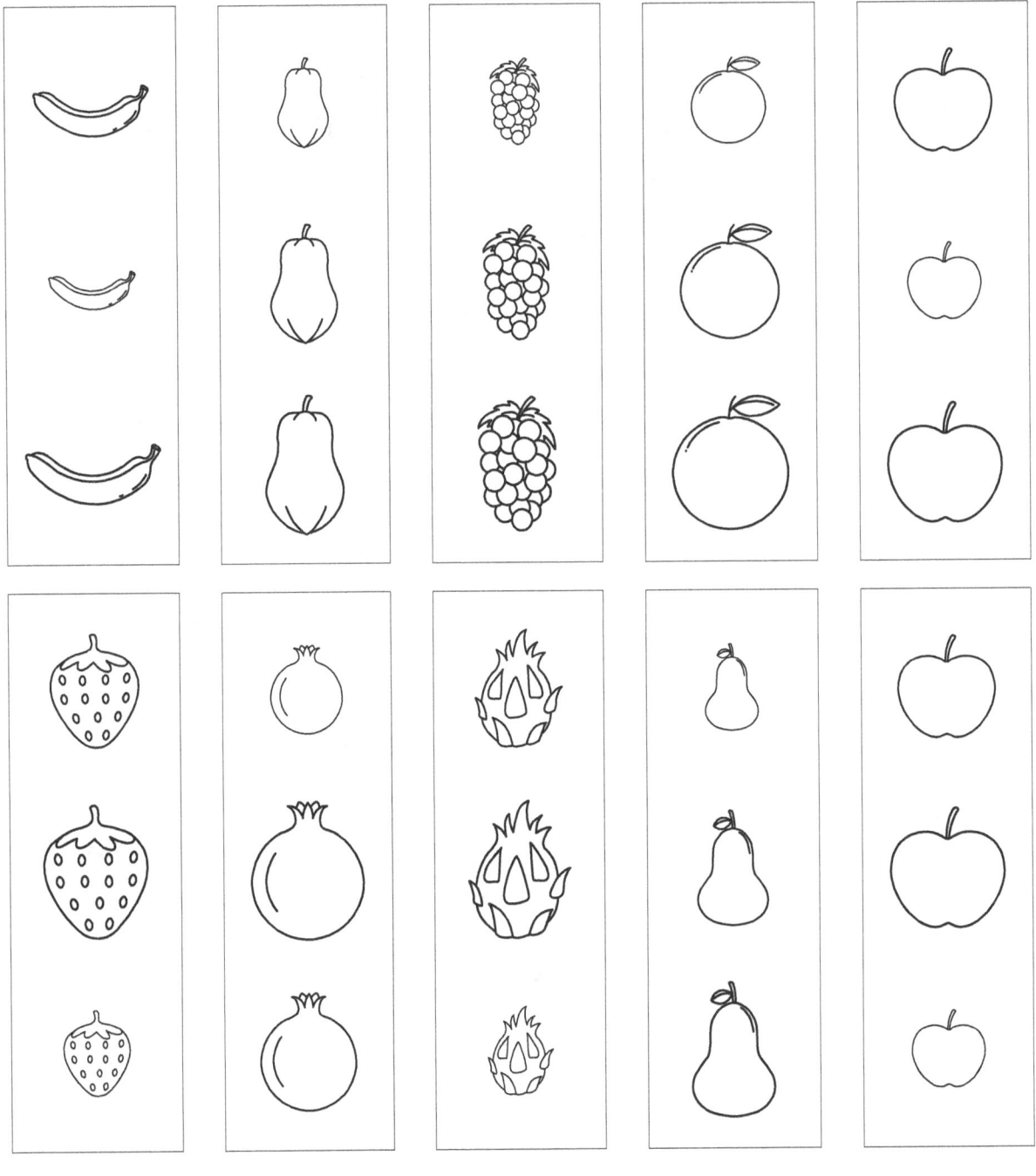

Heaviest and lightest

Check the heaviest and cross out the lightest object.

Which is lighter?

Identify and circle the lighter object.

More vs less

Check the group that is more and cross that is less.

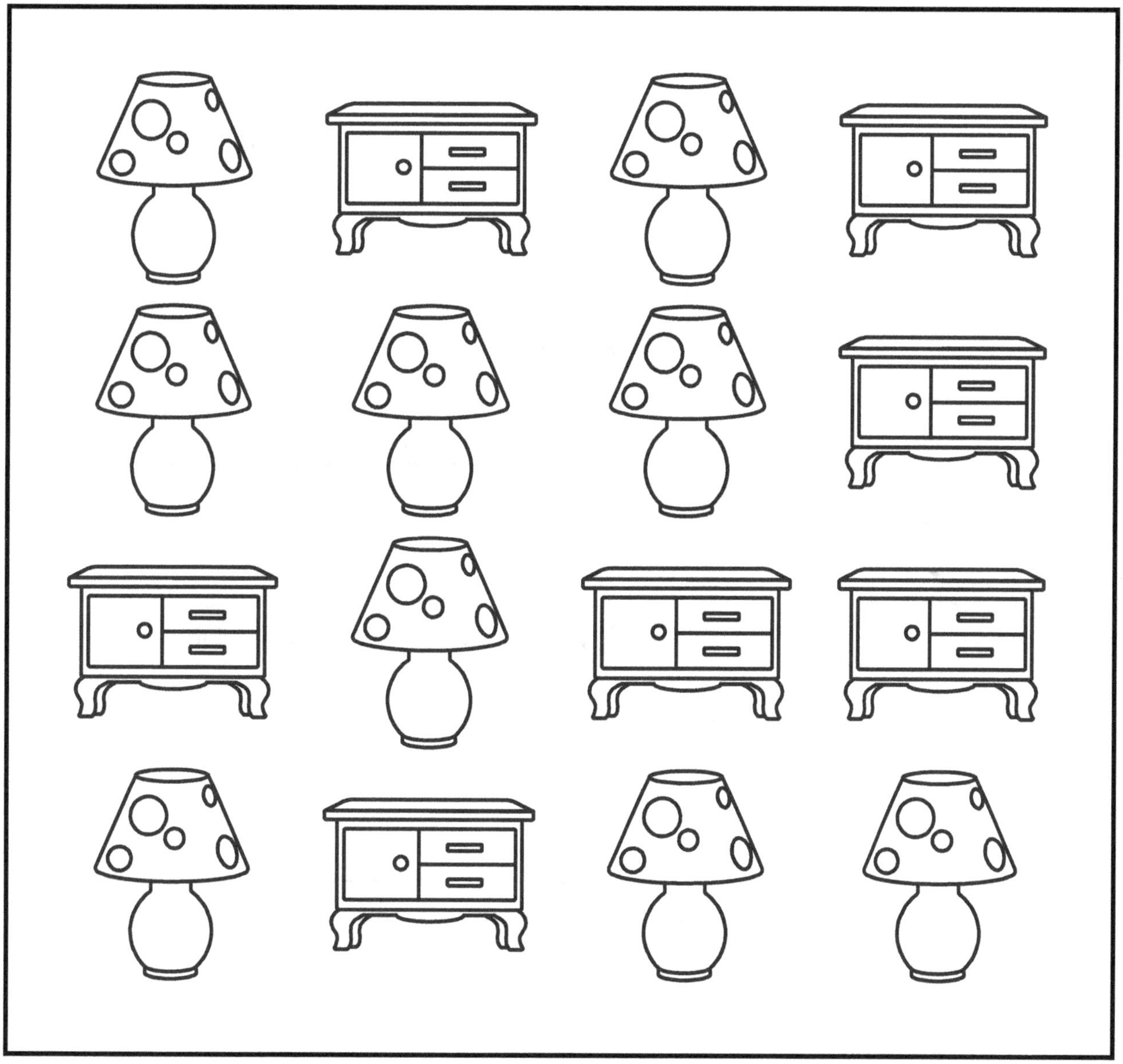

 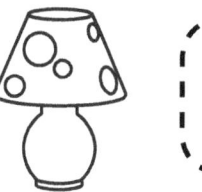 

Tallest and shortest

Check the tallest and put an X on the shortest item.

Order by length

Order from the shortest to longest object.

Which is the largest?

Identify the largest object

Longest and shortest

Check the longest and cross out the shortest object.

Which is taller?

Identify and circle the taller image.

Find the Shortest

Draw a rectangle around the shortest object.

More vs less

Find the item that is more and item that is less.

1)
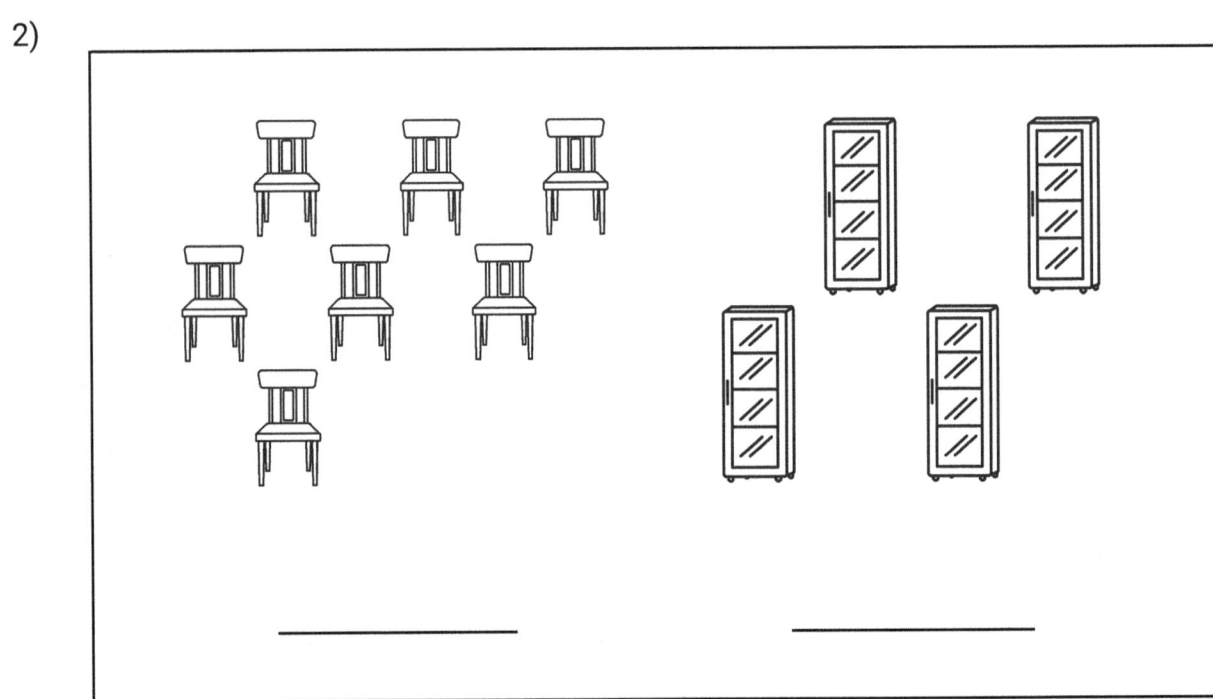

2)

More vs less

Find the item that is more and item that is less.

1)

_____   _____

2)

_____   _____

More vs less

Find the item that is more and item that is less.

1)
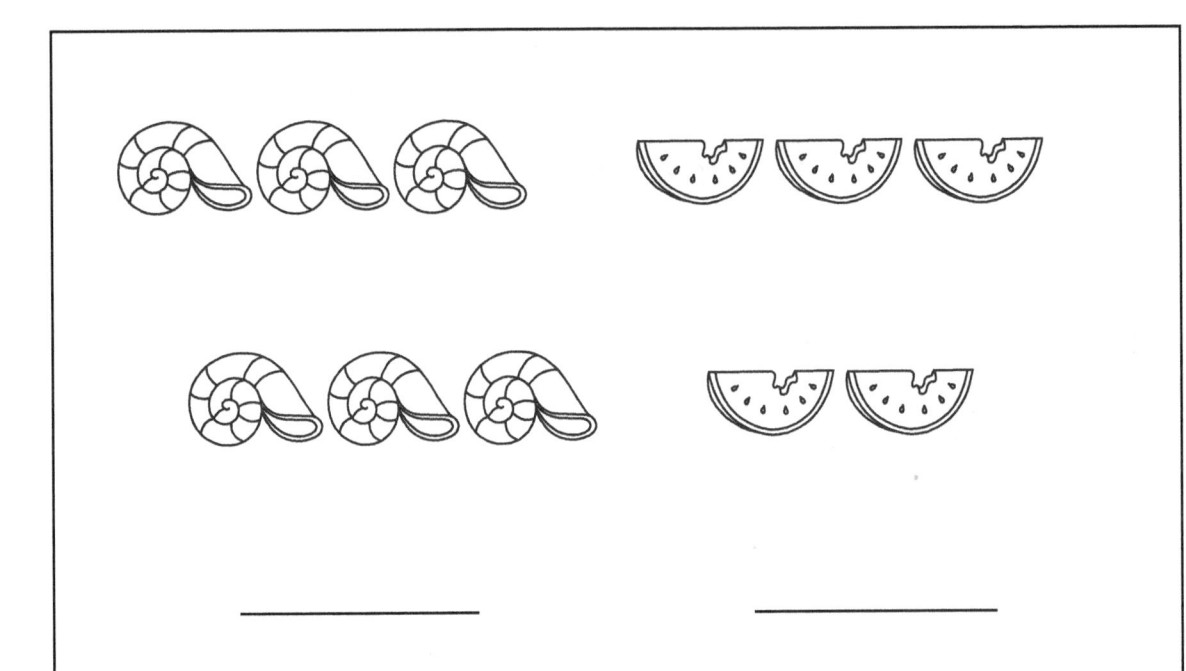

2)

Heaviest and lightest

Check the heaviest and cross out the lightest object.

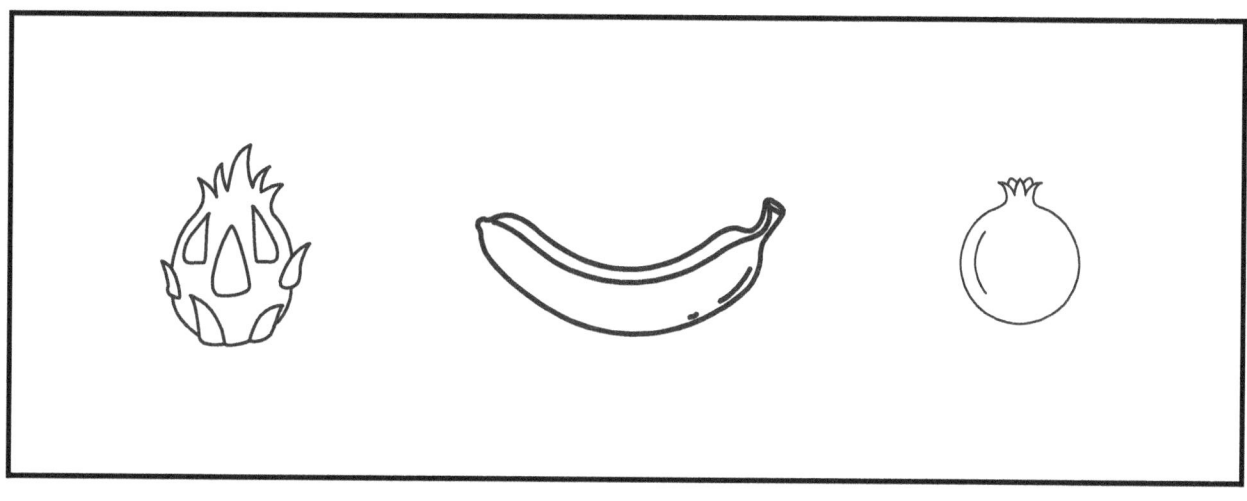

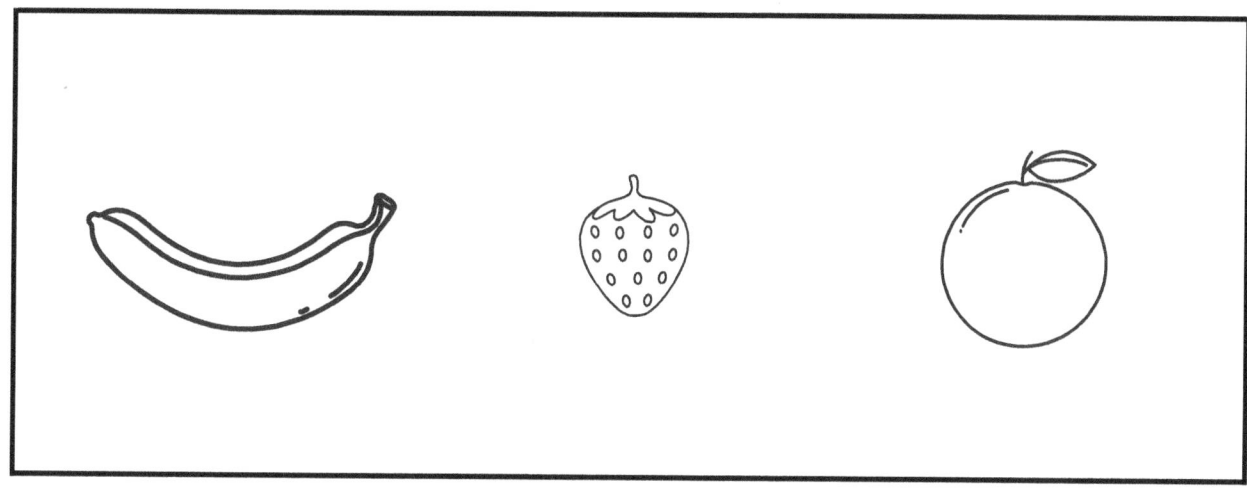

Heaviest and lightest

Check the heaviest and cross out the lightest object.

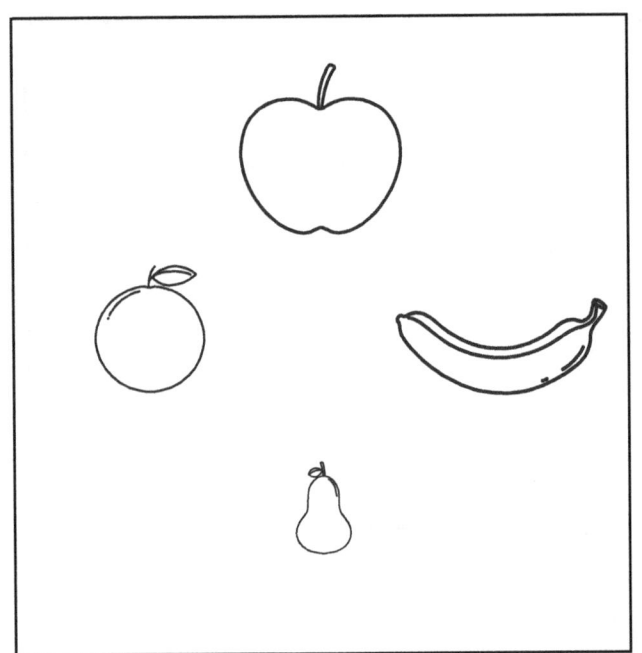

More vs less

Find the item that is more and item that is less.

1)

2)

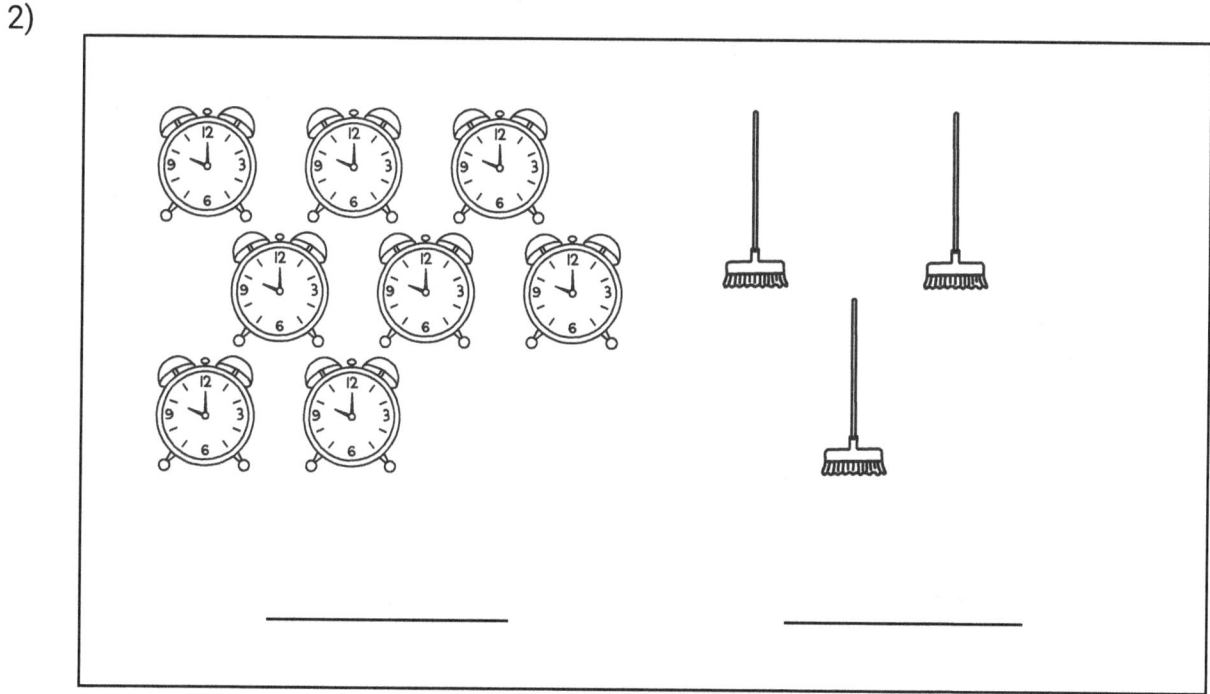

More vs less

Find the item that is more and item that is less.

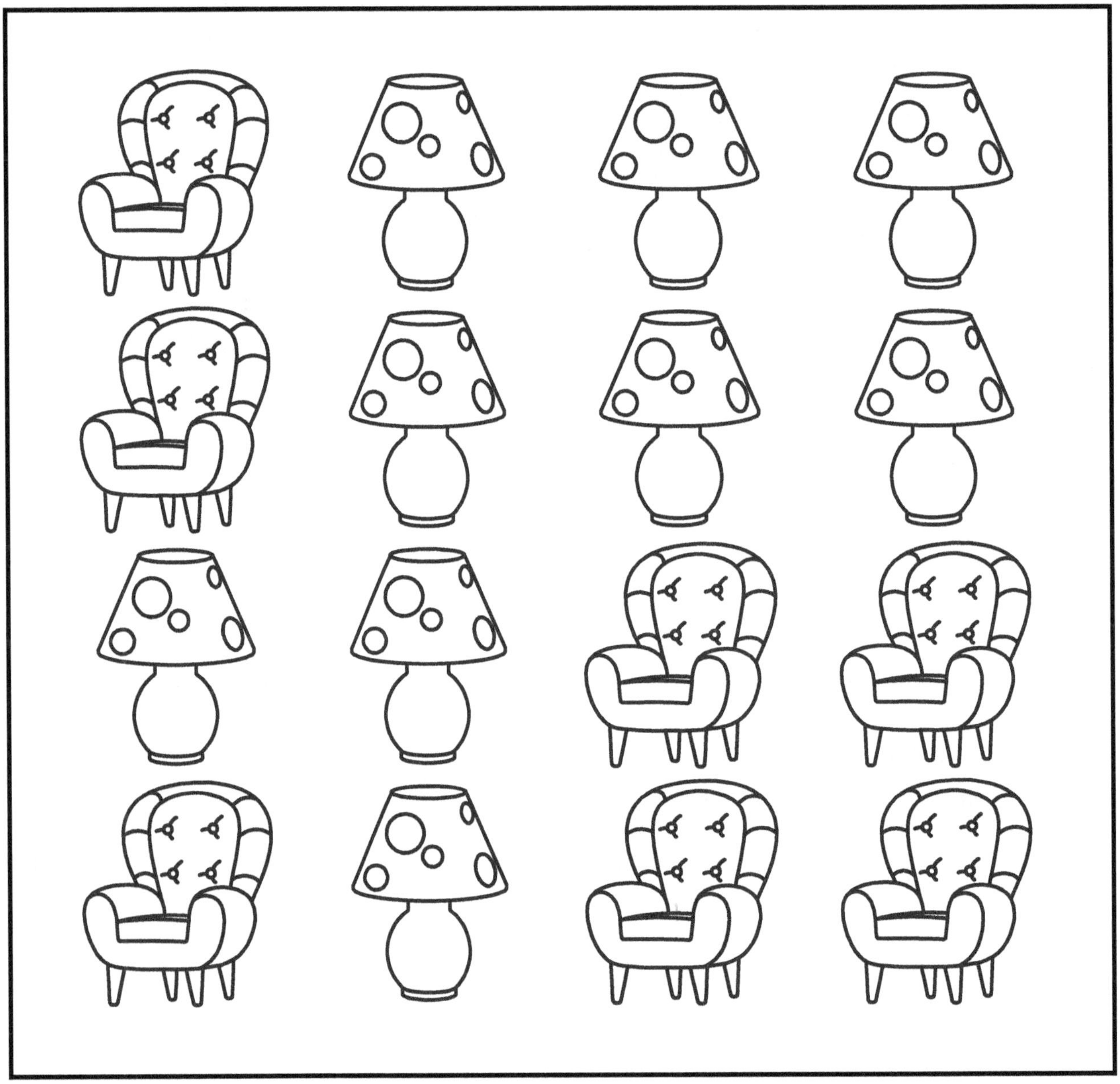

 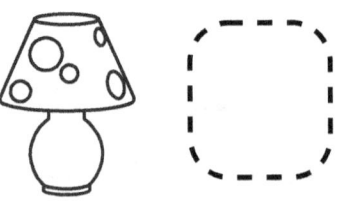

More vs less

Find the item that is more and item that is less.

1)

_____   _____

2)

_____   _____

Tallest and shortest

Check the tallest and cross the shortest item.

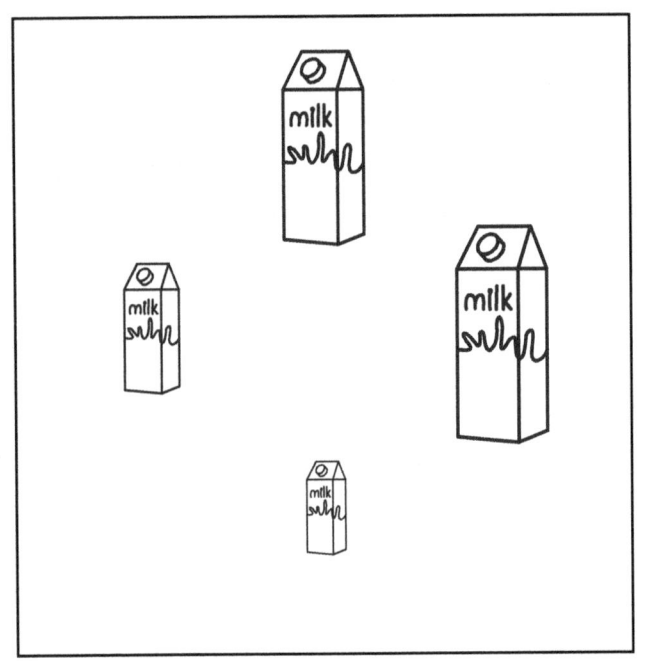

Order by weight

Order the images from lightest to heaviest.

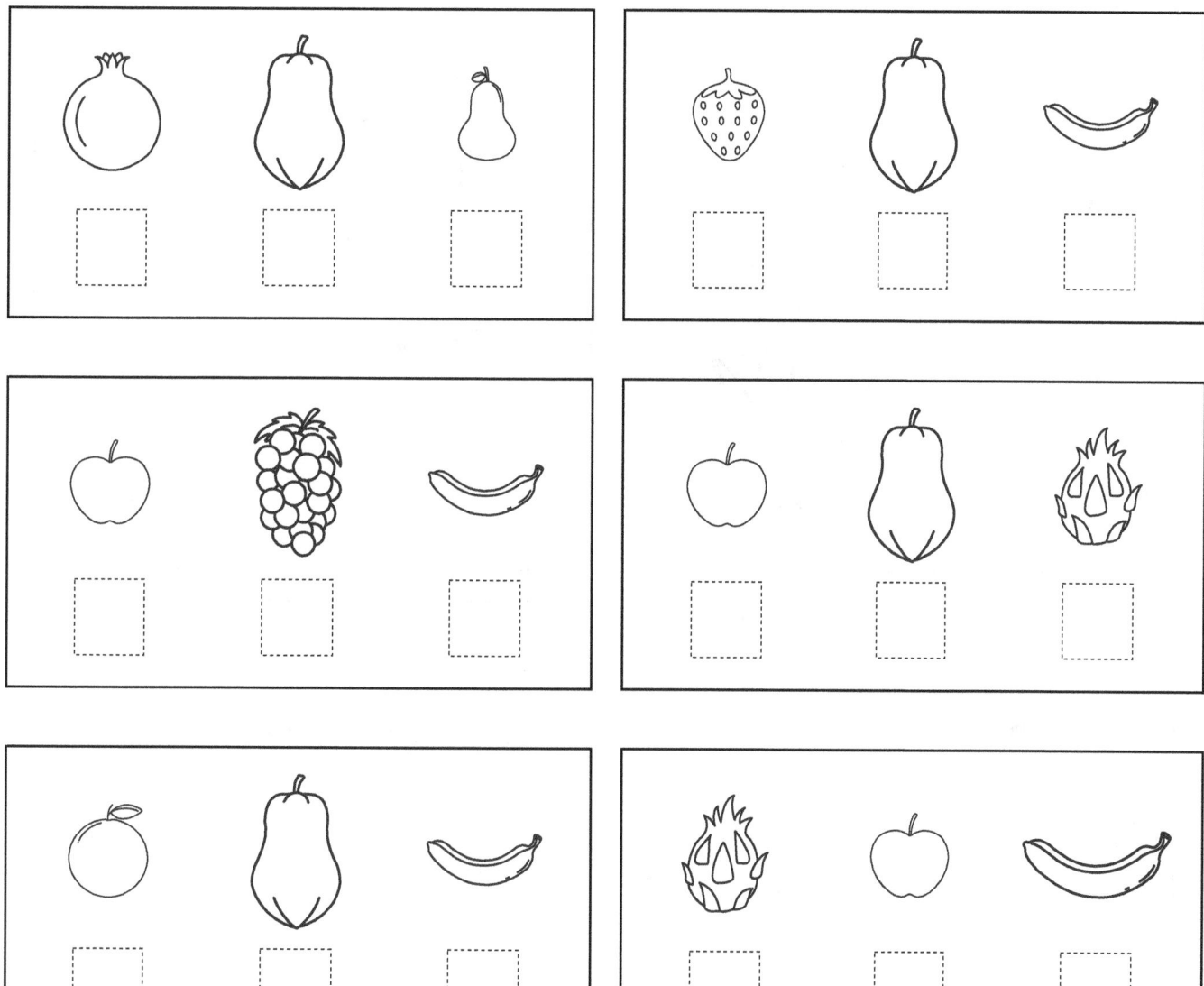

Which is heavier?

Identify and circle the heavier object.

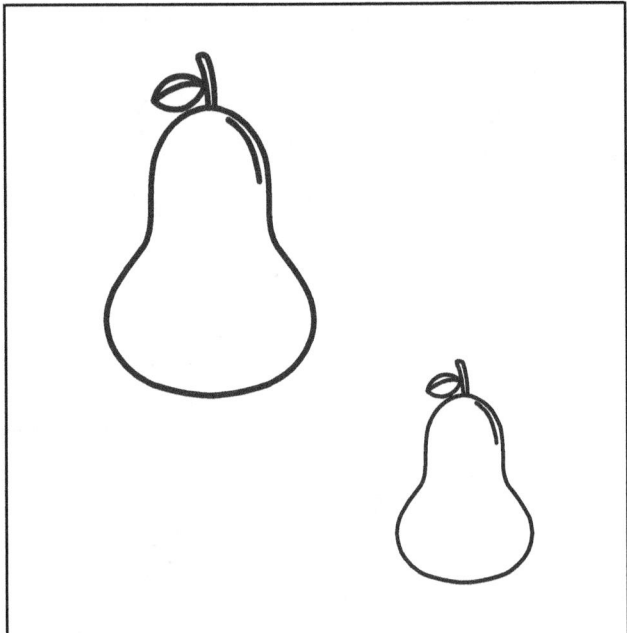

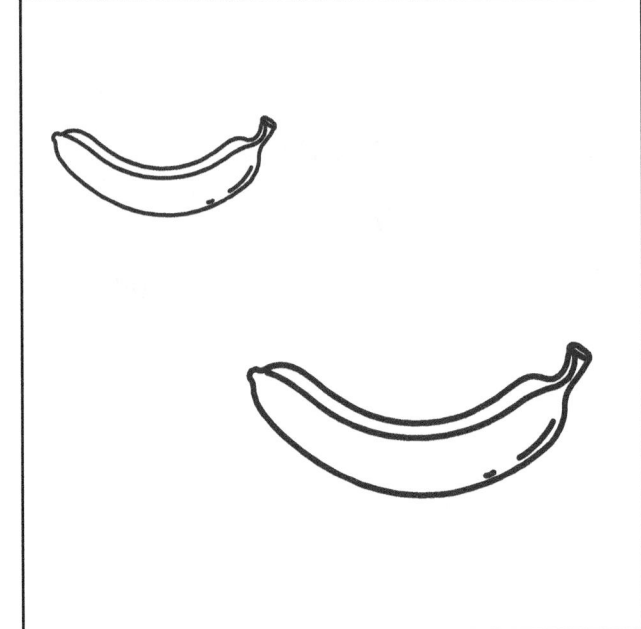

Which is shorter?

Identify and circle the shorter object.

Order By height

Order the objects from shortest to tallest.

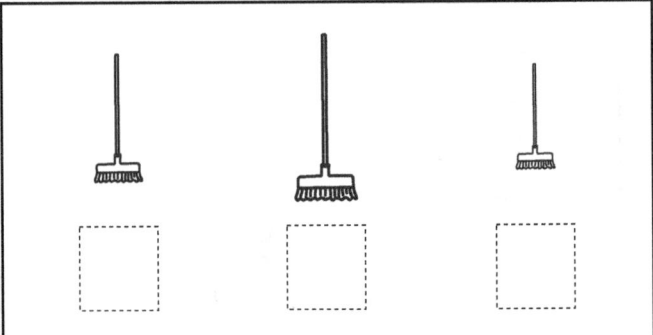
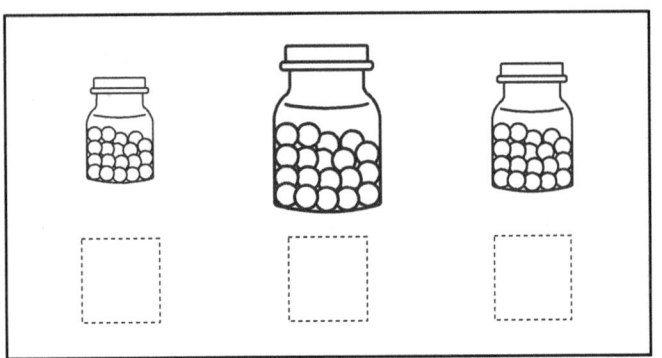
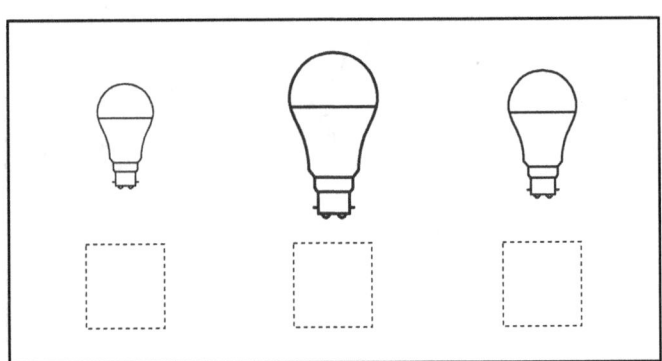
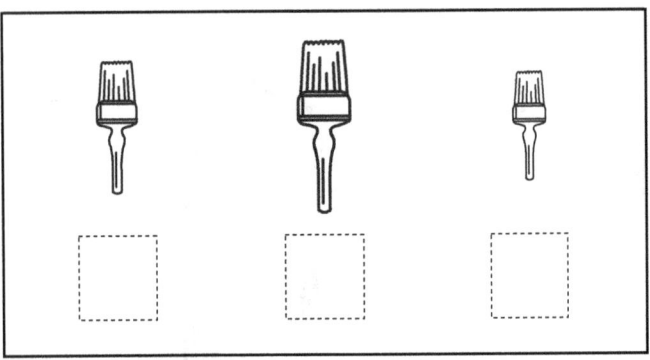
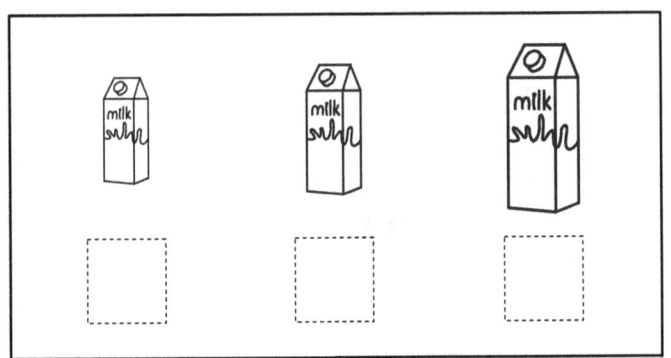

Heaviest and lightest

Circle the heaviest and cross out the lightest object.

Which is shorter?

Identify and circle the shorter object.

Longest and shortest

Cross out the longest and circle the shortest object.

More vs less

Check the group that is more and cross that is less.

1)

2)

More vs less

Find the item that is more and item that is less.

1)

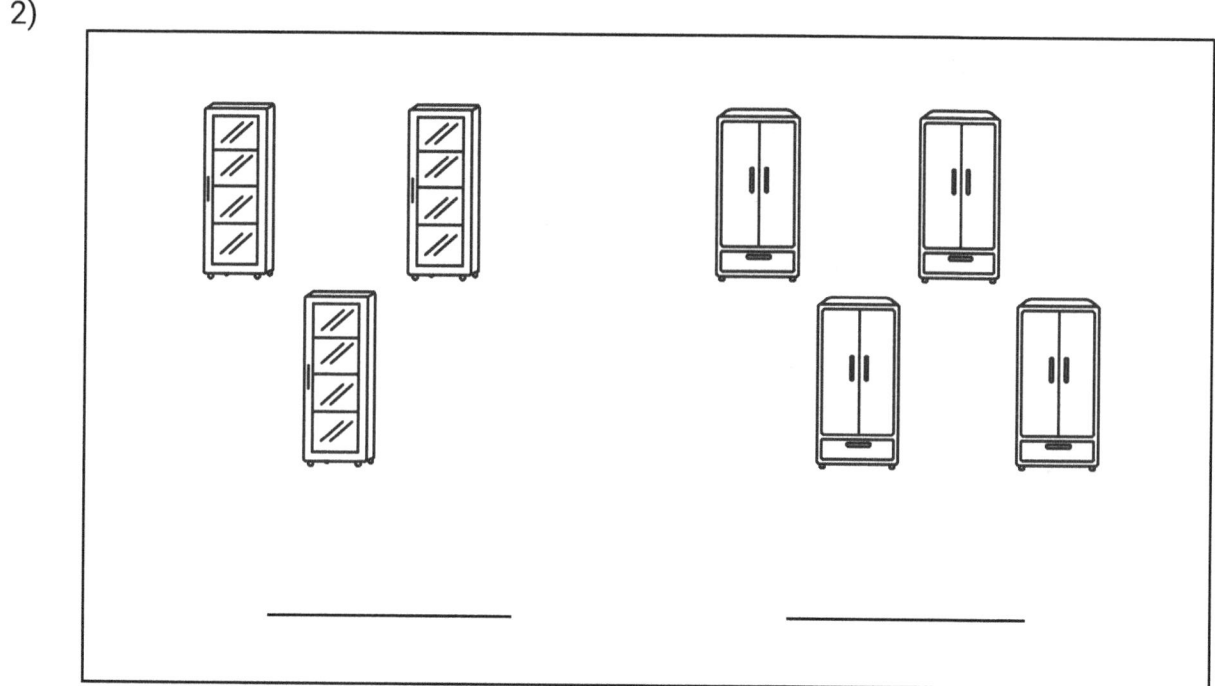

2)

More vs less

Find the item that is more and item that is less.

1)

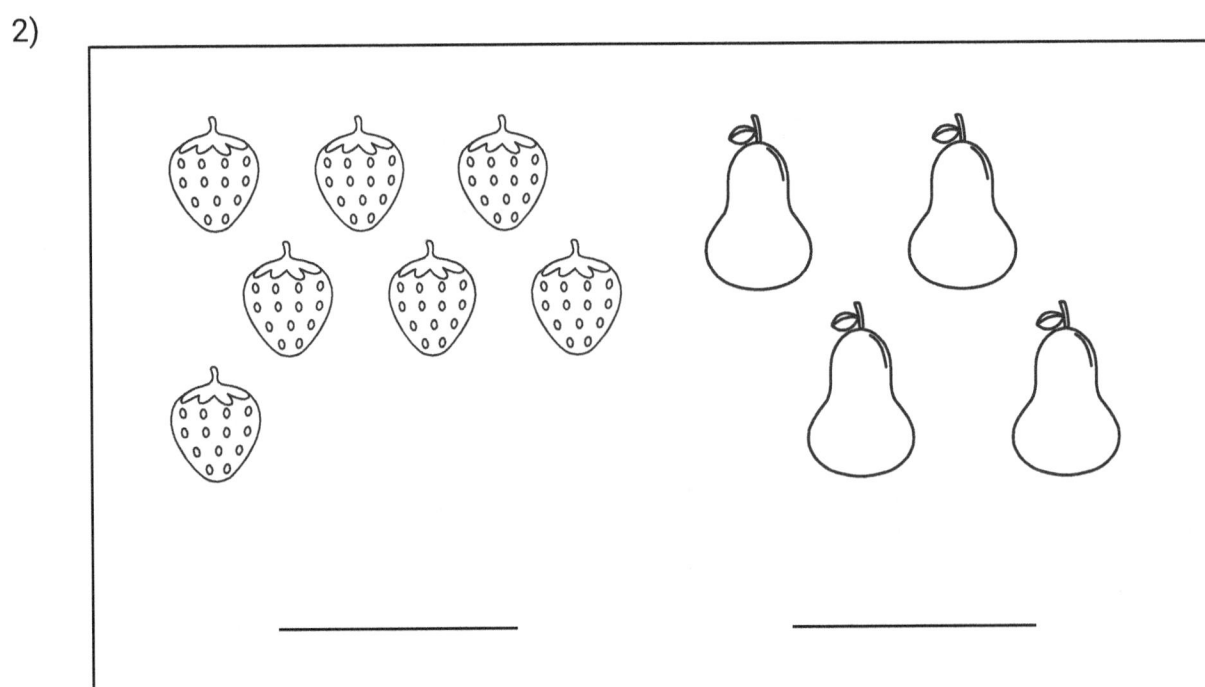

2)

_____   _____

More vs less

Find the item that is more and item that is less.

1)

2)

Big vs Small

Cross out the biggest item and circle the smallest one.

Heaviest and lightest

Cross out the heaviest and circlet the lightest object.

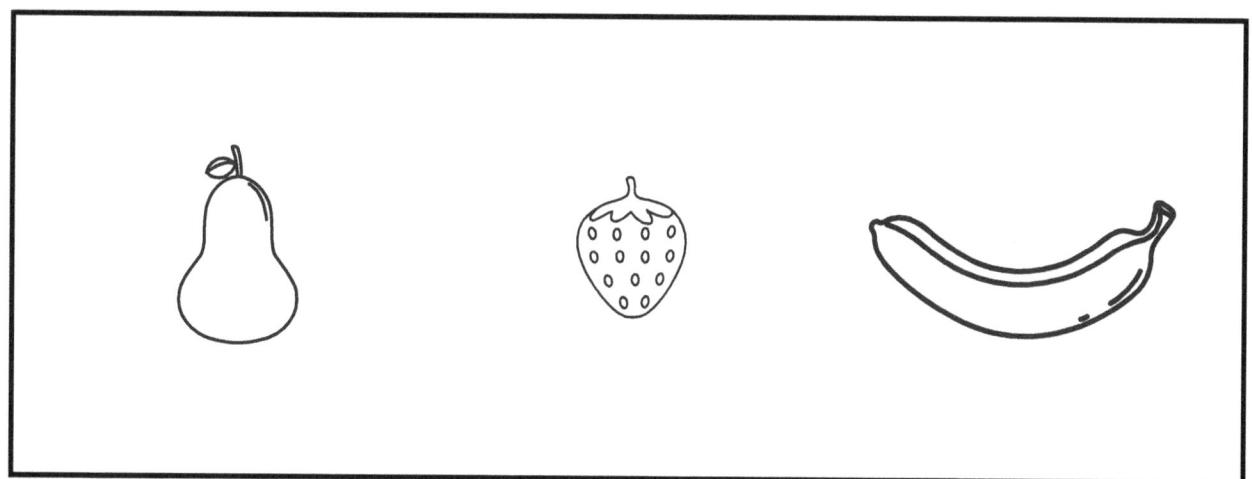

Heaviest and lightest

Check the heaviest and cross out the lightest object.